INGLÉS PARA NIÑOS

I SPEAK ENGLISH TOO! 1

ISBN: 978-1-914911-16-3

www.zigzagenglish.co.uk

ZIGZAG ENGLISH

OUR BOOKS FOR CHILDREN
www.zigzagenglish.co.uk

Our bilingual books for young children. Funny stories in simple, useful everyday English, with colour photos.
English with Tony -1- Tony moves house
English with Tony -2- Tony is happy
English with Tony -3- Tony's Christmas
English with Tony -4- Tony's holiday
My Best Friend

Our coursebook for child beginners (age 7 to 11)
English for Children - 1st Coursebook (Essential vocabulary and grammar for beginners)

Our series of dialogue books for beginners (for beginners aged 7 - 11). With word lists, comprehension questions, speaking tasks and more.
I Speak English Too! - 1
I Speak English Too! - 2

Our series of reading and comprehension books for beginners (for beginners aged 7 - 11). With word lists, comprehension questions and more.
Read English with Zigzag - 1
Read English with Zigzag - 2
Read English with Zigzag - 3
Read English with Zigzag 1, 2 and 3
　　　Audiobook - Books 1 + 2 (Audible)

The Learn English Activity Book for Children *(A1 - A2, elementary). (Recommended for children in early secondary school.)*

Our series of reading and comprehension books for children at elementary level (recommended for ages 10 - 13). With word lists, comprehension and discussion questions and lots of language activities.
Read English with Ben - 1
Read English with Ben - 2
Read English with Ben – 3

Our series of reading and discussion books (with writing tasks) *for children at secondary school, A2 - B1*
I Live in a Castle – Book 1 – The Choice
I Live in a Castle – Book 2 – The New Me

The Speak English, Read English, Write English Activity Books – *3 books from A1 to B2, for older children and adults.*

Our non-fiction book with language activities
Learn English with Fun Facts! – A2 – B2

English Dialogues for Secondary School – for ages 11 to 17, A2 – B2

OUR BOOKS FOR ADULTS

Our 3 Grammar books with grammar-focused dialogues
Learn English Grammar through Conversation – A1, A2 and B1

Our Dialogue books for adults (with vocabulary lists and comprehension questions)
50 very Easy Everyday English Dialogues (A2)
50 Easy Everyday English Dialogues (A2 - B1)
50 Intermediate Everyday English Dialogues (B1 - B2)
50 more Intermediate Everyday English Dialogues (B1 - B2)
40 Advanced Everyday English Dialogues (B2 – C1)
40 Intermediate Business English Dialogues (B1 - B2)
40 Advanced Business English Dialogues (B2 - C1)

Our activity books for adults and older children
The Speak English, Read English, Write English Activity Books – 3 books, for A1 - A2, A2 - B1 and B1 – B2.

Our non-fiction book with language activities
Learn English with Fun Facts! – A2 – B2

Contents

Los objetivos de este libro son:

1. Dar a su hijo la confianza necesaria para leer y hablar en inglés.
2. Enseñarle palabras y frases clave y gramática para ayudarle a mejorar su uso del inglés.

Nuestro método para enseñar inglés a niños de primaria:

1. Estos diálogos fueron escritos por una profesora de inglés titulada y con experiencia y comprobado en niños de 7 a 12 años.
2. La forma más rápida de aprender un idioma es de manera individual. Si habla un poco de inglés, puede utilizar este libro para enseñarle a su hijo. No se preocupe por cometer errores - basta con leer las oraciones y las listas de vocabulario que aparecen en el libro. No obstante, puede llevar las cosas más allá utilizando los diálogos para crear y mantener nuevas conversaciones con su hijo.
3. Por supuesto, los diálogos también son aptos para hermanos y hermanas.
4. Este libro empieza por lo más básico y luego añade palabras y frases para mejorar el inglés de su hijo. El niño tiene la oportunidad de aprender más con los diálogos "llenando los espacios" y con las preguntas de comprensión. También se pone a prueba el vocabulario en sopas de letras.
5. En 23 diálogos, su hijo pasará de "Hello. What's your name?" a saber decir "Can you buy Christmas presents there? I want to buy presents for my family."
6. ¡Y luego estará listo para pasar al Libro 2!

Cómo usar este libro:

1. Lea el diálogo A con su hijo.
2. Revisen la lista de vocabulario juntos.
3. Cambien roles y lean el diálogo nuevamente.
4. Anime a su hijo a realizar el ejercicio. La actividad "Fill the Gaps" puede hacerse sin ver las oraciones originales - este es un reto divertido, que permitirá al niño utilizar cualquier palabra que tenga sentido dentro del diálogo. O lo que es más fácil, puede pedirle a su hijo que vea las oraciones que faltan - están al final del ejercicio - y que escoja las correctas. Las respuestas a las preguntas de comprensión de los diálogos 2, 4, 6, 8 y 10 se

encuentran al final del libro.

5. Lean el <u>diálogo B</u>. Cambien roles. Hágale a su hijo las preguntas de <u>C: "What about you?"</u>

6. Si usted habla inglés, intente conversar con su hijo utilizando el lenguaje en los diálogos A y B, así como el lenguaje de diálogos anteriores. Por supuesto también puede incluir algunas palabras y frases nuevas si así lo desea. Desde nuestro punto de vista, esta es la manera más efectiva de enseñarle inglés a un niño. Ayudará a su hijo a mejorar su uso del inglés día a día.

7. A medida que el inglés de su hijo mejore, intente incluir algunos libros y audiolibros sencillos y animar a su hijo a ver televisión para niños. ¿Por qué no prueba nuestra serie de 3 libros de lectura progresiva en inglés para principiantes: **Read English with Zigzag**? Trata sobre un gato, un perro, un hermano y una hermana. ¡Es divertido y tiene muchos dibujos! También incluye listas de vocabulario, preguntas de comprensión y actividades lingüísticas.

8. Continúe con el <u>Libro 2</u> para ayudar a su hijo a alcanzar el siguiente nivel.

9. Ver a un niño pasar de no entender nada a ser capaz de llevar una conversación real es maravilloso. ¡Buena suerte y diviértanse!

LESSON 1

1A: Hello! Where do you live?

Anna: Hello.

Katie: Hello. What's your name?

Anna: My name's Anna. What's your name?

Katie: I'm Katie. How are you?

Anna: I'm fine. How are you?

Katie: I'm okay, thank you. How old are you?

Anna: I'm ten. How old are you?

Katie: I'm nine. You're big! I'm small. My sister is big.

Anna: What's your sister's name and how old is she?

Katie: Her name is Jessica. She's eleven.

Anna: Where do you live?

Katie: I live in **the UK**. I live in **Cambridge**. Where do you live?

Anna: I live in Madrid, in Spain. Madrid is big. Is Cambridge small?

Katie: It's not **very** small, but it's not very big. Do you like Madrid?

Anna: Yes, I do. I like it. It's **nice**. Goodbye, Katie.

Katie: Bye, Anna.

Vocabulary
- the UK — el Reino Unido
- Cambridge – a city in the south east of England
  una ciudad del sureste de Inglaterra
- very — muy
- nice — bonito

1A: Fill the gaps

Anna: Hello.

Katie:

Anna: My name's Anna. What's your name?

Katie:

Anna: I'm fine. How are you?

Katie:

Anna: I'm ten. How old are you?

Katie:

Anna: What's your sister's name and how old is she?

Katie:

Anna: Where do you live?

Katie:

Anna: I live in Madrid, in Spain. Madrid is big. Is Cambridge small?

Katie:

Anna: Yes, I do. I like it. It's nice. Goodbye, Katie.

Katie:

1. *I live in the UK. I live in Cambridge. Where do you live?*
2. *Bye, Anna.*
3. *I'm Katie. How are you?*
4. *It's not very small, but it's not very big. Do you like Madrid?*
5. *Her name is Jessica. She's eleven.*
6. *I'm okay, thank you. How old are you?*
7. *Hello. What's your name?*
8. *I'm nine. You're big! I'm small. My sister is big.*

1B

Sam: Hello!

Jack: Hello. I'm Jack. What's your name?

Sam: My name's Sam and my **big brother's** name is Andrew.

Jack: Are you okay?

Sam: Yes, I'm fine. How are you?

Jack: I'm okay, thanks.

Sam: Are you eleven?

Jack: No, I'm not. I'm not eleven, I'm ten. How old are you? You're big!

Sam: I'm eleven. I live in Cambridge. Do you live in Cambridge too?

Jack: Yes, I do. I live in Cambridge too. Cambridge is small.

Sam: Yes, it's **quite** small.

Jack: Bye, Sam.

Sam: Goodbye, Jack!

Vocabulary
- big brother   hermano mayor
- quite   bastante

1C: What about you?

1. *What's your name?*
2. *How are you?*
3. *Where do you live?*

LESSON 2

2A: My mum's English and my dad's Spanish

Anna: Hello Katie. How are you **today**?

Katie: Hi Anna. I'm fine, thanks. Is that your mum?

Anna: Yes, it is.

Katie: What's your mum's name?

Anna: Her name's Claire.

Katie: Is she nice?

Anna: Yes, she's very nice.

Katie: Is your mum Spanish?

Anna: No, she's not. My dad's Spanish, but my mum's not. She's English.

Katie: Does your dad **speak** English?

Anna: No, he doesn't. My mum speaks English and Spanish. My dad speaks Spanish, but he doesn't speak English.

Katie: My mum and dad are English. They speak English. I speak English and **a little bit** of Spanish.

Anna: Do you really speak Spanish? That's great!

Vocabulary
- today   hoy
- to speak   hablar
- a little bit   un poco

2A: Find the right answer

1. Is Anna's mum Spanish?
   a. No, she's not, she's English.
   b. Yes, she is. She's Spanish.
   c. No, she's not, she's American.

2. Does Anna's mum speak Spanish?
   a. No, she doesn't, she speaks English.
   b. Yes, she does, she speaks Spanish and English.
   c. She speaks a little bit of Spanish.

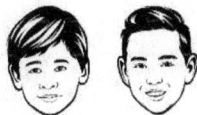

2B

Jack: Hi, Sam.

Sam: Hi!

Jack: Are you okay?

Sam: Yes, I'm fine, thanks.

Jack: Is that boy your brother?

Sam: Yes, he's my big brother. His name's Andrew.

Jack: How old is he?

Sam: He's quite big. He's twelve.

Jack: Do you like him?

Sam: Yes, I do. I quite like him. He's okay. Do you have a brother?

Jack: No, I don't. But I have a little sister. She's very small. She's five.

Sam: Do you like her?

Jack: No, I don't. I don't like her. She's too small. She's **boring**.

Vocabulary
- boring   aburrido

2C What about you?

1. *What's your mum's name?*
2. *Is your dad English?*
3. *Does your mum speak English?*

LESSON 3

3A: I like it

Katie: What do you like, Anna? Do you like **ice cream**?

Anna: Yes, I do. I like ice cream **a lot**.

Katie: I like ice cream too. I like ice cream and chocolate.

Anna: I like ice cream, I like chocolate, and I like chocolate ice cream!

Katie: What don't you like?

Anna: I don't like **peas**. I **really** don't like them!

Katie: Do you like your **house**?

Anna: Yes, I do. My house is very nice. It's quite big.

Katie: I like my bedroom. It's quite small, but I like it.

Anna: What colour is your bedroom?

Katie: It's green.

Anna: Green is a nice colour. Is it your **favourite** colour?

Katie: No, it's not. I like green, but my favourite colour is red.

Anna: I like green and red too. My favourite colour is orange. My bedroom is blue, but my **bed** is orange. I love it!

Vocabulary

- ice cream   helado
- a lot   mucho
- pea   guisante
- really   realmente
- house   casa
- favourite   favorito
- bed   cama

3A: Fill the gaps

Katie: What do you like, Anna? Do you like ice cream?

Anna:

Katie: I like ice cream too. I like ice cream and chocolate.

Anna: I like ice cream, I like chocolate, and I like chocolate ice cream!

Katie: What don't you like?

Anna:

Katie:

Anna: Yes, I do. My house is very nice. It's quite big.

Katie: I like my bedroom. It's quite small, but I like it.

Anna:

Katie: It's green.

Anna: Green is a nice colour. Is it your favourite colour?

Katie:

Anna: I like green and red too. My favourite colour is orange. My bedroom is blue, but my bed is orange. I love it!

1. *Do you like your house?*
2. *No, it's not. I like green, but my favourite colour is red.*
3. *What colour is your bedroom?*
4. *I don't like peas. I really don't like them!*
5. *Yes, I do. I like ice cream a lot.*

3B

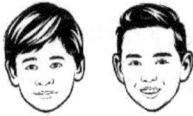

Sam: Do you have a dog, Jack?

Jack: No, I don't. **But** I have a very nice cat.

Sam: What colour is your cat? Is it black and white?

Jack: No, it's not. It's brown and white. Do you have a cat **too**?

Sam: No, I don't have a cat. My dad doesn't like cats. But I have a dog.

Jack: Do you have a big dog or a small dog?

Sam: It's not very big. It's quite small.

Jack: What colour is it?

Sam: It's black.

Jack: What's its name?

Sam: Its name is Fluffy.

Jack: Fluffy is a nice name. I like dogs. I **want** a dog.

Sam: You want a dog and I want a cat!

Vocabulary
- but   pero
- too   también
- to want   querer

3C What about you?

1. *What do you like?*
2. *What don't you like?*
3. *Do you have a cat?*
4. *Do you want a dog?*

LESSON 4

4A: Friends

Katie: **How many** friends do you have, Anna?

Anna: I have quite a lot of friends. I have six or seven friends. Do you have a lot of friends?

Katie: No, I don't. I have three friends.

Anna: Do you have a **best friend**?

Katie: Yes, I do. My best friend's name is Ben.

Anna: I have a best friend too. Her name's Sara. She's ten.

Katie: What does she **look like**?

Anna: She's very **tall**. She's quite **thin**.

Katie: Ben is **short**. He's a bit **fat**. He's a very nice boy. I like him a lot.

Anna: How many brothers and **sisters** does he have?

Katie: He has two brothers and two sisters. He has a big **family**.

Anna: Sara has a small family. She has no brothers or sisters. But she has a lot of friends.

Katie: Does she speak English?

Anna: She speaks a little bit of English. And a lot of Spanish!

Vocabulary

- how many   cuántos
- best friend   mejor amigo
- to look like   parecer
- tall   alto
- thin   delgado
- short   bajo
- fat   gordo
- sister   hermana
- family   familia

4A: Find the right answer

1. What is Anna's best friend's name?
   a. It's Ben
   b. Her best friend's name is Sara.
   c. She doesn't have a best friend.

2. Does Sara speak English?
   a. Yes, she speaks a lot of English.
   b. No, she doesn't speak English.
   c. Yes, she speaks a little bit of English.

3. How many friends does Anna have?
    a. She has three friends.
    b. She doesn't have a lot of friends.
    c. She has quite a lot of friends.

4. How many brothers and sisters does Ben have?
    a. He has a big family. He has three brothers and two sisters.
    b. He has no brothers or sisters. His family's small.
    c. He has four brothers and sisters.

5. Is Sara short and thin?
    a. Yes, she is. She's short and thin.
    b. No, she's not. She's short and fat.
    c. She's thin, but she's not short.

4B

Sam: Do you like my big brother, Jack?

Jack: Your brother Andrew? Yes, I do. He's nice. I like him. He's very tall, isn't he?

Sam: Yes, he's quite tall. What does your little sister look like?

Jack: She's not tall. She's very short. She's quite fat. She has **long** brown hair. She has big brown eyes.

Sam: Andrew has short **fair** hair and blue eyes.

Jack: You have short fair hair too. But you don't have blue eyes. You have brown eyes, don't you?

Sam: Yes, I do. What's your sister's favourite colour?

Jack: It's yellow. She likes yellow a lot. What's Andrew's favourite colour?

Sam: I don't know.

Vocabulary
- long   largo
- fair   rubio

4C What about you?

1. *How many friends do you have?*
2. *Do you have a best friend?*
3. *What does your friend look like?*
4. *What's your friend's favourite colour?*

LESSON 5

5A: Sara's house

Katie: **Where** does your best friend live, Anna?

Anna: My friend Sara?

Katie: Yes. Does she live in Madrid?

Anna: Yes, she does. She lives **near** my house.

Katie: What's her house like? Does she live in a big house?

Anna: No, she doesn't. Her house isn't very big, because she has a small family. But it's quite nice. It has a **beautiful garden**.

Katie: How many **bedrooms** does her house have?

Anna: It has two bedrooms. Does your house have two bedrooms too?

Katie: No, there are three bedrooms in my house. One for me, one for my sister and one for my **parents**.

Anna: What's your **living room** like?

Katie: We have a **lovely** living room. It has a big blue sofa and an **enormous television**. The living room is my favourite room.

Vocabulary
• where	donde
• near	cerca de
• beautiful	hermoso
• garden	jardin
• bedroom	dormitorio
• parent	padre
• living room	sala de estar
• lovely	bonito
• enormous	enorme
• television	televisión

5A: Fill the gaps

Katie: Where does your best friend live, Anna?

Anna: My friend Sara?

Katie: Yes. Does she live in Madrid?

Anna:

Katie: What's her house like? Does she live in a big house?

Anna:

Katie: How many bedrooms does her house have?

Anna:

Katie: No, there are three bedrooms in my house. One for me, one for my sister and one for my parents.

Anna: What's your living room like?

Katie:

1. *No, she doesn't. Her house isn't very big, because she has a small family. But it's quite nice. It has a beautiful garden.*
2. *We have a lovely living room. It has a big blue sofa and an enormous television. The living room is my favourite room.*
3. *It has two bedrooms. Does your house have two bedrooms too?*
4. *Yes, she does. She lives near my house.*

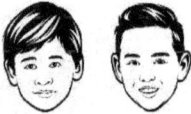

5B

Sam: Where do you live, Jack? Is your house near here? Is it near the **park**?

Jack: No, it's not. It's near the big Tesco's supermarket.

Sam: I live quite near the park. Not **far** from the **cinema**.

Jack: What's your house like?

Sam: I live in a **flat**. It's very small. It has two bedrooms – one for my parents and one for me and my brother.

Jack: Does it have a nice living room?

Sam: No, not really. The living room is **tiny**.

Jack: Do you have a garden?

Sam: No, we don't. But we live near the park, so that's okay.

Vocabulary

- park · parque
- supermarket · supermercado
- far · lejos
- cinema · cine
- flat · piso
- tiny · muy pequeño

5C What about you?

1. *Where does your friend live?*
2. *What's your friend's house like?*
3. *How many bedrooms does your house have?*
4. *Does it have a nice living room?*

LESSON 6

6A: Two pets

Katie: Do you like animals, Anna?

Anna: Yes, **of course** I do. I love animals.

Katie: Do you have a **pet**?

Anna: Yes, I have two pets. I have a **rabbit** and a **hamster**.

Katie: Why do you have a rabbit AND a hamster?

Anna: Because one pet isn't **enough**. I don't want a rabbit OR a hamster – I want **both**!

Katie: Do your parents like your two pets?

Anna: No, not really. But my friends like them.

Katie: Hamsters are okay; but I don't like rabbits.

Anna: Why not? Why don't you like them?

Katie: Because they **bite**!

Vocabulary

• of course	por supuesto
• pet	mascota
• rabbit	conejo
• hamster	hámster
• enough	suficiente
• both	ambos
• to bite	morder

6A: Find the right answer

1. Does Anna hate animals?
    a. No, she doesn't. She quite likes animals.
    b. She doesn't hate them but she doesn't like them.
    c. Of course not! She loves animals!

2. How many pets does Anna have?
    a. She has one pet. It's a cat.
    b. She has two pets – a rabbit and a hamster.
    c. She doesn't have any pets.

3. Who likes Anna's pets?
      a. Her parents like them.
      b. Her friends like them.
      c. Katie likes them.

6B

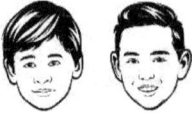

Jack: I really want a dog, Sam.

Sam: Don't you have a cat?

Jack: Yes, I do. I like my cat, but I want a dog too.

Sam: Dogs are nice, but they're very **messy**.

Jack: Cats aren't messy. But they're a bit boring.

Sam: Cats are beautiful. I want a cat, but my dad doesn't want one.

Jack: Does your mum want a cat?

Sam: Yes, she does. She likes cats a lot. But my dad really doesn't like them.

Jack: Does your brother like cats **or** dogs?

Sam: He likes **snakes**.

Jack: Snakes? I **hate** snakes!

Vocabulary
- messy   desordenado
- or   o
- snake   serpiente
- to hate   odiar

C What about you?

1. *Do you have a pet?*
2. *Do you like animals?*
3. *Does your mum like snakes?*

Word Search 1

```
W K V V G A G Y P T Y W F L V
I G M A Q F A X E T E T M J C
H T A I V O R U T I N Y Q B H
D U P Y B N D U S Q E G U O O
M G C L O V E L Y E A G I R C
P E W U S E N E F R R R T I O
R I M Z H R Y S H O R T E N L
K C H K I Y A T I P L M W G A
N H M R N K E A D A V M A W T
Q Y C Y G T A U L R R W J Y E
S W F W W L I V R E X F Z E Y
H Z D D Y B L U K N Y U B R L
F A V O U R I T E T B C P Q I
O R I V H Z B S A S Y A X Y C
V T V H O Y H N Y M H B U T W
```

- I love  , but I don't like ice cream.
- Your mum and dad are tall, but my **p_re_t_** are **s_or_**.
- I don't like your house. It's too small – it's **t_ny**! But your **g_rd_n** is **l_ve_y**!
- My best friend has a **_er_** nice **p_t**. It's a cat.
- What's your **fa_our_te** pet? Dogs. Hamsters are **q_it_** nice too, but rabbits are **b_r_ng**.
- Do you live **n_ar** the cinema?

LESSON 7

7A: What time is it?

Katie: What time is it in Madrid, Anna?

Anna: It's nine o'clock.

Katie: Nine o'clock? It's eight o'clock **here**. It's **early**.

Anna: Do you have school today?

Katie: No, I don't. Are you at school?

Anna: Yes, I am.

Katie: What time do you **go to school**?

Anna: I **get up** at half past seven. I go to school at half past eight. I **start** school at nine o'clock.

Katie: I start school at a quarter to nine. I get up at eight o'clock, and **run** to school! Do you **walk** to school?

Anna: Yes, I walk to school. It's near my house.

Vocabulary
- here   aquí
- early   temprano

- to go to school — ir a la escuela
- to get up — levantarse
- to start — empezar
- to run — correr
- to walk — caminar

7A: Fill the gaps

Katie: What time is it in Madrid, Anna?

Anna:

Katie: Nine o'clock? It's eight o'clock here. It's early.

Anna:

Katie: No, I don't. Are you at school?

Anna:

Katie: What time do you go to school?

Anna:

Katie: I start school at a quarter to nine. I get up at eight o'clock, and run to school! Do you walk to school?

Anna:

1. *Yes, I am.*
2. *Do you have school today?*
3. *Yes, I walk to school. It's near my house.*
4. *I get up at half past seven. I go to school at half past eight. I start school at nine o'clock.*
5. *It's nine o'clock.*

7B

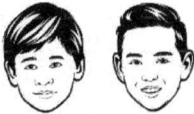

Sam: Do you like school, Jack?

Jack: No, not really. School starts too early. It starts at ten to nine.

Sam: That *is* early. My school starts at a quarter past nine.

Jack: What time is your **lunch break**?

Sam: We have lunch at twenty to one.

Jack: And **when** do you go **home**?

Sam: At a quarter to four.

Jack: That's quite **late**. We go home at five past three.

Sam: When do you **do your homework**?

Jack: I don't have a lot of homework. My mum **drives** me to school, and I do my homework in the **car**!

Vocabulary
- lunch break   pausa del almuerzo
- when   cuando
- home   casa
- late   tarde
- to do homework   hacer los deberes
- to drive   conducir
- car   coche

7C What about you?

1. *What time is it?*
2. *What time do you go to school?*
3. *What time do you have lunch?*
4. *Do you walk or run to school?*
5. *Do you have a lot of homework?*

LESSON 8

8A: It's cold

Anna: Is it cold in Cambridge? It's not cold in Madrid. **It's quite warm**.

Katie: It's cold here. My house is quite cold. But my school is too **hot**.

Anna: Where are you? Are you at school?

Katie: No. I'm in my bedroom.

Anna: I'm in my bedroom too.

Katie: Is your sister **there**?

Anna: No, she's in the **kitchen**. But my friend Sara is here.

Katie: Where are your pets?

Anna: My rabbit's here, in my bedroom. But my hamster is in my sister's bedroom.

Katie: Does your sister like your hamster?

Anna: Yes, she loves my hamster. She wants my hamster to live in her bedroom. But she doesn't really like my rabbit.

Katie: Why not? Does your rabbit bite?

Anna: **Maybe** a little bit.

Vocabulary
- cold   frío
- it's warm / hot   hace calor
- there   allí
- kitchen   cocina
- maybe   tal vez

8A: Find the answers

1. Is it cold in Madrid?
   - a. Yes, it is. It's quite cold.
   - b. No, it's not. It's quite warm.
   - c. Yes, it is. It's cold and rainy.

2. Where's Sara?
   - a. She's at home.
   - b. She's in Cambridge.
   - c. She's in Anna's bedroom.

3. Why doesn't Anna's sister like her rabbit?
   - a. Because it bites.
   - b. Because it's boring.
   - c. Because it's not a hamster.

8B

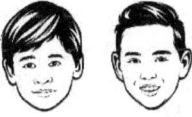

Sam: It's really cold today.

Jack: It's **always** cold in Cambridge.

Sam: No, it's not; not always.

Jack: When it's not cold, it **rains**.

Sam: No; **sometimes** it's hot and **sunny**.

Jack: I'm cold. I'm very cold.

Sam: Do you want to go home?

Jack: Yes, I do. Do you want to **come** to my house?

Sam: Is your house cold too?

Jack: No, it's not. It's really warm in my house.

Sam: Great! **Let's go!**

Vocabulary
- always   siempre
- to rain   llover
- sometimes   a veces
- sunny   soleado
- to come   venir
- let's go   vamos

8C What about you?

1. *Is it cold today? Or is it hot and sunny?*
2. *Where are you?*

LESSON 9

9A: What's your school like?

Anna: What's your school like, Katie? Is it nice?

Katie: It's okay. I quite like it. Do you like your school?

Anna: Yes, I do. It's a very good school.

Katie: How big is the school?

Anna: It's big. There are **about** five **hundred children**.

Katie: **How many** boys and how many girls are there?

Anna: I don't know. But there are fifteen girls and ten boys in my **class**.

Katie: That's a lot of girls.

Anna: Yes. Do you have a lot of girls in your class?

Katie: No. **Half** my class are boys.

Anna: Is your best friend in your class?

Katie: No. He doesn't go to my school. He goes to a **different** school.

Anna: Oh, that's bad **luck**.

Vocabulary

• about	alrededor de
• hundred	cien
• children	niños
• how many	cuántos
• class	clase
• half	la mitad
• different	diferente
• luck	suerte

9A: Fill the gaps

Anna:

Katie: It's okay. I quite like it. Do you like your school?

Anna:

Katie: How big is the school?

Anna:

Katie: How many boys and how many girls are there?

Anna:

Katie: That's a lot of girls.

Anna:

Katie: No. Half my class are boys.

Anna:

Katie: No. He doesn't go to my school. He goes to a different school.

Anna:

1. *I don't know. But there are fifteen girls and ten boys in my class.*
2. *Oh, that's bad luck.*
3. *Yes, I do. It's a very good school.*
4. *Is your best friend in your class?*
5. *It's big. There are about five hundred children.*
6. *Yes. Do you have a lot of girls in your class?*
7. *What's your school like, Katie? Is it nice?*

9B

Sam: What are the **teachers** like at your school?

Jack: They're not bad. We have **some** very good teachers.

Sam: **What's your teacher called**?

Jack: She's called Mrs Brown. Her **husband works** at the school too.

Sam: What does he do? Is he a teacher too?

Jack: No. He's a **cook**. He cooks our school **lunches**.

Sam: Is he a good cook?

Jack: I **think** so. We have a lot of **fish and chips**. I love fish and chips!

Sam: I don't have school lunches. I **take** sandwiches to school.

Jack: Don't you think sandwiches are boring?

Sam: Yes, they are a bit boring. I have **cheese** sandwiches **every day**!

Vocabulary

- teacher — profesor
- some — algunos
- what's…called? — ¿cómo se llama?
- husband — marido
- to work — trabajar
- cook — cocinero
- lunch — almuerzo
- to think — pensar
- fish and chips — pescado y patatas fritas
- to take — llevar
- cheese — queso
- every day — todos los días

9C What about you?

1. *How big is your school?*
2. *How many children are there in your class?*
3. *What's your teacher called?*
4. *Do you take sandwiches to school?*

LESSON 10

10A: Clothes

Anna: Does your school have a uniform, Katie?

Katie: Yes, of course it does. Don't **all** schools have a school uniform?

Anna: No. My school doesn't. Lots of schools in Spain don't.

Katie: Really? **Lucky** you! I hate my school uniform.

Anna: **Why** do you hate it? What is your uniform?

Katie: Girls and boys all wear black **trousers**, a white **shirt** and a purple top.

Anna: That sounds okay. What's wrong with that?

Katie: Some girls don't like trousers. They want to wear **skirts**.

Anna: So do the boys like the uniform?

Katie: No, not really. Lots of boys don't like purple.

Anna: Why not? I love purple. I **often** wear purple tops to school.

Katie: **Seriously**?!

Vocabulary

• all	todos
• lucky you!	¡Qué suerte!
• why	por qué
• trousers	pantalones
• shirt	camisa
• skirt	falda
• often	a menudo
• seriously	en serio

10B

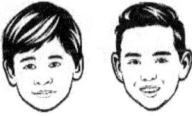

Sam: Do you like **shopping**, Jack?

Jack: Yes, I love shopping. I like **buying** new **clothes** with my mum.

Sam: **How often** do you buy new clothes?

Jack: Quite often. Maybe **once a month**.

Sam: I like new clothes too. But my mum says they're too **expensive**.

Jack: Some clothes shops are **cheap**. And buying online is cheap too.

Sam: I really want some new **trainers**. But the ones I like are very expensive.

Jack: Maybe **wait** till **Christmas**?

Sam: What do you want for Christmas?

Jack: I want a new **jacke**t. A beautiful red one. It's online.

Sam: Is it cheap?

Jack: No, not really. But it's for Christmas!

Vocabulary

• to shop	ir de compras / comprar
• to buy	comprar
• new	nuevo
• clothes	ropa
• how often	con qué frecuencia
• once a month	una vez al mes
• expensive	caro
• cheap	barato
• trainers	zapatillas de deporte
• to wait	esperar
• till	hasta
• Christmas	Navidad
• jacket	chaqueta

10A / 10B: Answer the questions
1. What is Katie's school uniform?
2. How often does Jack go shopping?

3. Does Jack want some new trainers for Christmas?

10C: What about you?

1. *Does your school have a uniform?*
2. *Do you like shopping?*
3. *What do you want for Christmas?*

LESSON 11

11A: Buying presents

Anna: It's almost Christmas!

Katie: Yes, it is. I want to buy my sister a **present**. But I don't know what to get her.

Anna: What does she want?

Katie: I don't know.

Anna: What does she like?

Katie: She likes clothes, **music** and animals.

Anna: Does she like dogs?

Katie: Yes, she loves them.

Anna: Why don't you get her a dog?

Katie: A dog? I really don't think my parents want a dog.

Anna: Okay. Maybe buy her a **dress** or a jacket.

Katie: They're too expensive. I don't have a lot of **money**.

Anna: Is it cold in Cambridge?

Katie: Yes, it's very cold.

Anna: What about a **hat**?

Katie: Good **idea**! Thanks!

Vocabulary
- present   regalo
- music   música
- dress   vestido
- money   dinero
- hat   sombrero

11A: Fill the gaps

Anna:

Katie: Yes, it is. I want to buy my sister a present. But I don't know what to get her.

Anna:

Katie: I don't know.

Anna:

Katie: She likes clothes, music and animals.

Anna:

Katie: Yes, she loves them.

Anna:

Katie: A dog? I really don't think my parents want a dog.

Anna:

Katie: They're too expensive. I don't have a lot of money.

Anna:

Katie: Yes, it's very cold.

Anna:

Katie: Good idea! Thanks!

1. *Is it cold in Cambridge?*
2. *What about a hat?*
3. *Does she like dogs?*
4. *What does she like?*
5. *It's almost Christmas!*

6. *Okay. Maybe buy her a dress or a jacket.*
7. *What does she want?*
8. *Why don't you get her a dog?*

11B

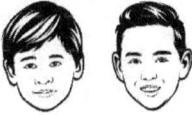

Sam: Do you want to go to the Christmas **market,** Jack?

Jack: **Where** is it?

Sam: It's in the **city centre**.

Jack: Is it good?

Sam: Yes, it's great. There are nice **things** to **eat** and **drink**.

Jack: Can you buy Christmas presents there? I want to buy presents for my family.

Sam: Yes, there are lots of things to buy.

Jack: Is it expensive?

Sam: I think it's quite expensive. But if you like, we can go to the **shops** too.

Jack: Yes, that **sounds good**. When do you want to go?

Sam: How about Saturday **afternoon**?

Jack: Yes, Saturday's good. **See you then**.

Vocabulary
- market   mercado
- where   donde
- city centre   centro de la ciudad
- thing   cosa
- to eat   comer
- to drink   beber
- shop   tienda
- sounds good   eso suena bien
- afternoon   por la tarde
- see you then   hasta luego

11C: What about you?

1. *What does your mum want for Christmas?*
2. *Is it cheap or expensive?*

LESSON 12

12A: Christmas

Katie: What's Christmas like in Spain?

Anna: It's great. We get presents. We see all our family and eat lots of food!

Katie: We eat lots of food too, and Father Christmas brings us presents on **Christmas Day**.

Anna: Do you go to **church** at Christmas?

Katie: My family doesn't.

Anna: My school has a Christmas **party**. I love it!

Katie: At schools in the UK, there's always a Christmas **play**. All the little children are in the play.

Anna: I hope you have a good Christmas, Katie.

Katie: You too, Anna. **Merry Christmas**!

Vocabulary
- Father Christmas   Papá Noel
- to bring   traer
- Christmas Day   Día de Navidad
- church   iglesia

- party   fiesta
- play   obra de teatro
- Merry Christmas!   ¡Feliz Navidad!

12B: What about you?

1. *What do you have to eat at Christmas?*
2. *Do you go to church at Christmas?*
3. *Does Father Christmas bring you presents?*

Word Search 2

```
Z D J H E P G R D L U N C H Z
I M Z K C D Z R J T Z J H N H
X C M P L B R C W Y P J E O I
J H O K T R A I N E R S A R N
V T E Q R L U C K Y F U P Q O
Y V A B O U T Z C Q Q N B K B
C R C H U R C H G C H N F Q A
V T P R S H B A L W A Y S E O
R A M D E A R L Y Y W J U N S
G W V Z R T M F Y H F X E P F
P D D V S M B W Q U V O Y P P
G D F H L O P Z U F V Z D S A
V H K C U W A U B W T Q B L B
H A D W S D Z P S A Q Q J Y Z
N Y E Q Y N D W U H O M E S G
```

- My school doesn't have a uniform. I wear **tr_in_rs** and **tr_us_rs** to school.
- Do you **a_w_ys** have **l_n_h** at school, or do you sometimes eat it at **h_m_**?
- You're **l_c_y**! You start school late. But I start school **_ar_y**.

- On Sunday, we go to at **ab_ut h_lf** past ten.
- It sometimes rains in the summer. But it's often **s_n_y**.
- I want to buy a **_hea_** present for my friend, because I don't have a lot of money.

Respuestas

Dialogue 2A: Find the right answer

1: a
2: b

Dialogue 4A: Find the right answer

1: b
2: c
3: c
4: c

Dialogue 6A: Find the right answer

1: c
2: b
3: b

Dialogue 8A Find the right answer

1: b
2: c
3: a

Dialogues 10A / 10B: Answer the questions

1. It's black trousers, a white shirt and a purple top.
2. He goes shopping about once a month.
3. No, he wants a new red jacket for Christmas.

```
W K V V G A G Y P T Y W F L V
I G M A Q F A X E T E T M J C
H T A I V O R U T I N Y Q B H
D U P Y B N D U S Q E G U O O
M G C L O V E L Y E A G I R C
P E W U S E N E F R R R T I O
R I M Z H R Y S H O R T E N L
K C H K I Y A T I P L M W G A
N H M R N K E A D A V M A W T
Q Y C Y G T A U L R R W J Y E
S W F W W L I V R E X F Z E Y
H Z D D Y B L U K N Y U B R L
F A V O U R I T E T B C P Q I
O R I V H Z B S A S Y A X Y C
V T V H O Y H N Y M H B U T W
```

```
Z D J H E P G R D L U N C H Z
I M Z K C D Z R J T Z J H N H
X C M P L B R C W Y P J E O I
J H O K T R A I N E R S A R N
V T E Q R L U C K Y F U P Q O
Y V A B O U T Z C Q Q N B K B
C R C H U R C H G C H N F Q A
V T P R S H B A L W A Y S E O
R A M D E A R L Y Y W J U N S
G W V Z R T M F Y H F X E P F
P D D V S M B W Q U V O Y P P
G D F H L O P Z U F V Z D S A
V H K C U W A U B W T Q B L B
H A D W S D Z P S A Q Q J Y Z
N Y E Q Y N D W U H O M E S G
```

Gracias por leer este libro.

Si tiene alguna pregunta sobre este libro, envíenosla y nos pondremos en contacto con usted lo antes posible. Si tiene alguna sugerencia para la próxima edición de este libro, o para otros libros que le gustaría que publicáramos para ayudar a su hijo a aprender inglés, nos encantaría escucharla.
Escríbanos a: lydiawinter.zigzagenglish@gmail.com

Puede echar un vistazo a nuestros otros libros para niños y adultos, jugar a algunos juegos en inglés y leer nuestro blog, en: **www.zigzagenglish.co.uk**.

Por favor...
Escribe una reseña sobre este libro. Las reseñas son importantes para otros padres y también para nosotros. Gracias.

Aquí tiene algunos extractos de nuestros otros libros para niños que empiezan a aprender inglés:

8A: A week's holiday

Katie: It's my **half term** holiday next week. A **whole** week with no school!

Anna: Are you going **away**?

Katie: Yes. We're going to the Lake District.

Anna: What's that? Where is it?

Katie: It's in the **north** of England. There are lots of **mountains** and **lakes**. It's very beautiful.

Anna: Lucky you! I have school next week.

Katie: School is really hard at the moment. I'm tired. I need a **break**.

Anna: Is your whole family going?

Katie: No. My mum has to work next week. So she's **staying** at home.

Anna: Your **poor** mum.

16. Too many boys and girls

Hi there! Is it your birthday today?

It's Poppy's birthday today. Poppy is nine today.

I don't like birthday parties. They're **noisy**. They're too noisy. There are lots of children. There are too many children.

Pam likes birthday parties. She likes noisy children. She likes eating birthday cake too.

I can't sit on my sofa. There are too many children in the living room! I can't eat my cat food. There are too many children in the kitchen! I can't look for a spider in the garden. That's **right** – there are too many boys and girls there!

Mum and Dad's bedroom is **quiet**. Their bed is quite comfortable.

See you tomorrow...

From: The Learn English Activity Book for children

CHOOSE!

You can't always have everything you want.
Sometimes you have to choose.
So what do you choose?

- Ice cream or chocolate?
- A hamster or a rabbit?
- Homework or **housework**?
- A holiday at the beach or a skiing holiday?
- One very good friend or three good friends?
- Football or swimming?
- A green bedroom or a white bedroom?
- Autumn or spring?
- Chinese food or Italian food?
- Very hot **weather** or very cold weather?
- Orange juice or a milkshake?